PUSSYFOOTING

Viv Quillin

KODANSHA INTERNATIONAL
New York • Tokyo • London

Kodansha America, Inc.
114 Fifth Avenue, New York, New York 10011, U.S.A.

Kodansha International Ltd.
17-14 Otowa 1-chome, Bunkyo-ku, Tokyo 112, Japan

Published in 1995 by Kodansha America, Inc.

First published in Great Britain in 1994 by Victor Gollancz, London.

Library of Congress Cataloging-in-Publication Data

Quillin, Viv, 1946–
    Pussyfooting : essential dance procedures for cats / Viv Quillin.
        p.   cm.
    Originally published: London : V. Gollancz, 1994.
    ISBN 1-56836-078-9
    1. Cats — Humor. 2. Ballroom dancing — Humor. 3. Ballet — Humor.
    4. Dance — Study and teaching — Humor. I. Title.
    PN6231.C23Q55 1995
    741.5′942 — dc20   94-31280

Printed in Hong Kong by Wing King Tong Company Limited

95 96 97 98 99   6 5 4 3 2 1

To all the wonderful pussycats in my life, both feline and human

"Dancing is the most fun you can have standing up"
Olivia Neutered-Tom

You can never begin too soon . . . teaching your kittens to dance.

For some, it is in the blood from birth.

BALLET

Being a ballet dancer involves a great deal of hard work, as shown by Monsieur Degas in one of his lesser-known paintings.

Marcia performing a near-perfect *à côtè*.

Hilary works on her *pirouette*.

And this is Sharon.

EACH DANCER WANTS TO LOOK HIS OR HER BEST

The bodice of the tutu must fit as tightly as possible at the waist so that it does not shift during lifts or supported *pirouettes*.

Baking Potatoes

Creak

Correctly fitting tutu.

Incorrectly fitting tutu.

LIFT TECHNIQUE

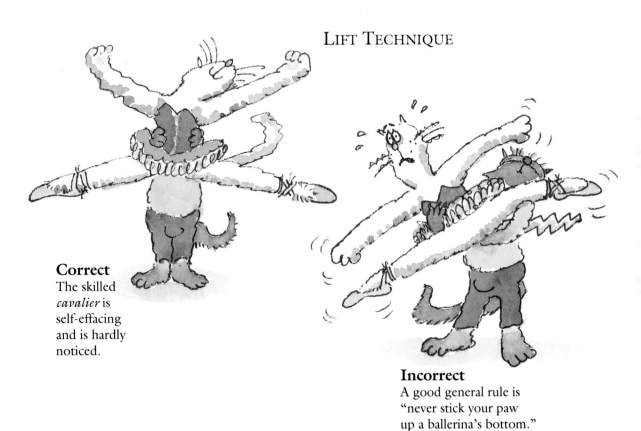

Correct
The skilled *cavalier* is self-effacing and is hardly noticed.

Incorrect
A good general rule is "never stick your paw up a ballerina's bottom."

Much work has to be
done at the barre before
a dancer is ready to
perform before an
audience.

Swan Lake with Odette danced by Fluffy and Prince Siegfried by Tibbles. The *corps de ballet* includes Sharon.

Slow Foxtrot – The Reverse Turn

Time 4/4
Tempo 30–32 bars per minute

Paw Turns
1. Step back with the RHP turning on it to the left.
2. Close the LHP back to the RHP, turning from the R to the L.
3. Step forward with the RHP.

*RHP Right Hand Paw
  LHP Left Hand Paw

Begin Here, Gentleman

Begin Here, Lady

L R   L R

Dance steps can look intimidatingly complex when you first begin.

But persevere – you may become another "Ginger" Rogers.

THE GENTLEMAN'S HOLD FOR MODERN BALLROOM

Stand in a relaxed yet upright position. Head should be naturally poised.

Raise the left front leg so that the paw is slightly above shoulder level. Bend leg so as to affect a graceful curve. The left front paw should hold the lady's right front paw with her palm downwards.

The right front paw should be just under the lady's left shoulderblade.

Both elbows should be kept well up without raising the shoulders.

THE LADY'S HOLD FOR MODERN BALLROOM

Stand in a natural yet upright position, looking over your partner's right shoulder. Raise the left front leg and rest the paw on the man's right upper front leg.

Ladies, do not try to lead or guide your partner. Just follow.

WRONG

RIGHT

BASIC BALLROOM FOR BEGINNERS

Shyer cats may prefer to learn the first dance steps in the privacy of their own home.

If you do not feel ready to handle a partner, choose a likely implement to dance with.

Move about the room using
the following rhythms:

Slow, slow, quick-quick, slow;
or, ONE-two-three,
ONE-two-three.

If you have begun to slow-dance
with the lights down low, it's
probably time to find a partner.

Driving Tips

The male steers the female firmly in a straight line across the room, swerving only for large furniture.

Cornering Taking firm hold of a handful of fur, swirl her around, tilted at an angle of 45 degrees. It is frighteningly easy to drop your partner on the floor at this point.

Here We Take You Through
One Cat's Journey to the Dance Floor

Fur maintenance is a
constant battle . . .

. . . and there is such a lot of it.

Fur volume can be controlled with a squirt of your owner's favorite hairspray. Alternatively, work in some cat food and leave to dry.

CHOOO!

Don't forget that dab of fish paste behind the ears.

THE MALE CAT ALSO HAS A COMPLEX SERIES OF PREPARATIONS FOR THE DANCE

Using a deodorant in anticipation of moving vigorously in a hot ballroom is no reflection on a cat's masculinity.

Applying gel to flatten obstinate fur will in no way affect your ability to sire kittens.

A soft brush will buff the top
hat nicely . . .

. . . but only the best will do
for shining your dancing shoes.

COMPETITION DANCING

For the cat who enjoys living on the edge, nothing beats competitive Tango. After months of practice hopeful entrants Debbie and Oscar are ready to perform.

Debbie
(6 months)
"I owe everything to the Pussy Foot School of Dancing."

Oscar
(9 months)
"I just want to get out there and win."

Procedure

1. The Tango is a deeply sensuous dance. Oscar is at his sultriest here.

2. "The Progressive Sidestep" Notice how Debbie's smile never slips.

3. Despite a small hernia,
Oscar executes a perfect
back corté

4. THE ATLANTIC CITY TANGO TOPSTERS!

Debbie: "I'd like to thank everyone . . .
especially my hairdresser."

Oscar: "I don't really know what to say."

Isadora Duncan's emotionally abandoned style of dancing swept America, the world, and many a cat into self-expression through movement.

Procedure

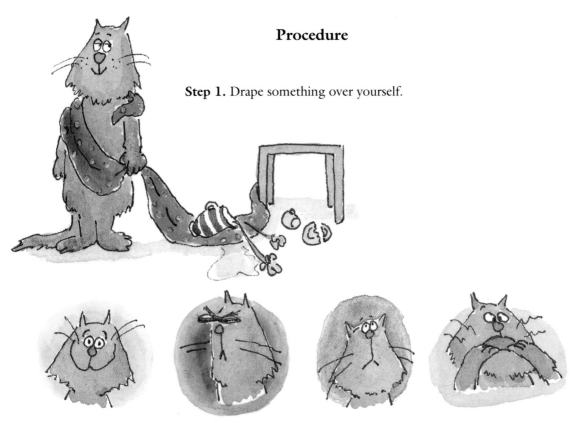

Step 1. Drape something over yourself.

Step 2. Arrange features into various intense expressions. Do three or four of these.

Step 3. Run around in an arty sort of way . . .

Step 4. . . . pausing now and again to really *feel*.

Step 5. Rest and become aware of the *Internal Life Force*.

Discover What Sort of Personality You Have from the Way You Dance

The Dance of the Seven Tails

PERSONALITY:
The Secretive Cat.

Enjoys creating mystery out of nothing. Often looks inscrutable for no reason. Favorite reading: anything by John Le Carré.

Performed by Madame Fluffy and her troupe.

The Sensuous Cat.

The dedicated sensuous kitty is prepared to desert food dish and fireplace in exchange for a good quality massage.

Procedure: Slip into something sleek (a fur coat?) and slide on to the dance floor. Lean against anything that moves. Purr heavily. Eyelids should remain at half mast throughout.

The Rumba

It is important for the female
to wear as little as possible . . . .

. . . Nevertheless,
points will be
knocked off if
underwear is visible.

The male *Rumbero* often forgets to
remove his hanger before dressing.
Another tricky problem is *panty line*.
Not to mention which side to dress
with the *tail*.

The Adventurous Cat.

Likes to cover a wide territory.
Has an owner in every port.

Sailor's Hornpipe

1. Act as if you are climbing a large tree.

2. Clutching stomach (think about throwing up a hair ball), stick out one back paw, then the other.

3. Weave front paw digits together. Clap underside of back paws vigorously without losing balance.

4. The graceful cat always lands on its paws.

PERSONALITY:

The Conformist.

We are looking at the cat who *likes* wearing school uniforms. This type is happiest with rules, routine, and a synchronized watch. A perfect puss for the formation dance team.

Unfortunately, any deviation from the "norm" stands out like a sore thumb. Try *not* to die of embarrassment mid-dance or you could look *really* conspicuous.

Formation Dancing

The Twist

Squirm-by-squirm instructions.

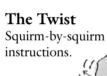

Imagine your tail is a bath towel and you are briskly drying your back . . .

. . . at the same time as you lower and raise your body.

Occasionally raise one back paw off the ground.

Remember to look as if you are enjoying yourself.

Originally performed in the sixties by Chubby Checker in a too-tight suit on TV night spots.

Now performed by over-sixties chubby cats in too-tight suits on senior citizen nights.

The Rowdy Cat.

If you are the sort of cat who enjoys communal singing late at night on a back garden wall, you will certainly enjoy the conga. You probably prefer package tours to a quiet ramble in the Maine woods.

The Conga

Procedure: Two steps forward, then stick your back paw out (preferably trip someone up or fall over at this point). Another two steps, then stick the other back paw out. No, not at the same time. Get up and continue, gripping the cat in front firmly. This often involves ripping something.

The Foxtrot

Procedure:
Dance with knees bent and long gliding steps. Be prepared to knee the odd groin if necessary.

PERSONALITY:
The cat who enjoys living dangerously. Never accept an invitation to go out on the patio and look at the moon afterward.

The Slow Waltz

PERSONALITY:
The "green" cat who likes to conserve energy by moving as little as possible. The dance floor is often packed for this number.

Procedure:
Lean heavily on partner, close eyes, and walk about very slowly to a vague one-two-three beat. You may lose the rhythm if you drop off to sleep. Save even more energy by avoiding partners with contrasting fur.

Country, Barn, and Square Dancing

EQUIPMENT:
Includes big sandals, kerchiefs round head or neck, flowery dresses with puffy sleeves, stetsons, cowboy boots, vests, anything in denim, aprons. Not necessarily all worn at once.

PERSONALITY:
You are extroverted and prefer lots of relationships on a superficial level rather than one or two intimate friends. You enjoy running about and knocking things over.

The Grand Chain

Dancers form a big circle. Facing your partner, clasp right paws. Toms always move round in a counterclockwise direction and queens vice versa. Change to left paws with next cat and right paws after that, etc. . . .

The Basket

You are strongly recommended to choose partners of a similar height for this swing step.

This advice also applies to "spinning" a partner in dances such as the Gay Gordon.

Do-Si-Do

Loud meows should be emitted frequently and
totally at random throughout any country dance.

The Funky Chicken

PERSONALITY:
The Gourmet (some would say food fixated). Often a Taurus, enjoys the pleasures of the flesh, particularly poultry.

Procedure:
Flap the forelegs like wings, meanwhile scratching the ground with a back leg (as if searching for worms, distasteful though the idea might be). In short, "make like a chicken and strut your stuff," as they say. Try not to drool.

Hippy Hippy shake

This cat is a snuggler. If there is not a human or other living being to cuddle up with, it will rub the fridge with affection. In desperate circumstances it will befriend a table leg.

Procedure:
Imagine a flea has been inserted under your fur at the top end and is working its way downward to emerge at the tip of your tail.

Ice Dancing

PERSONALITY:

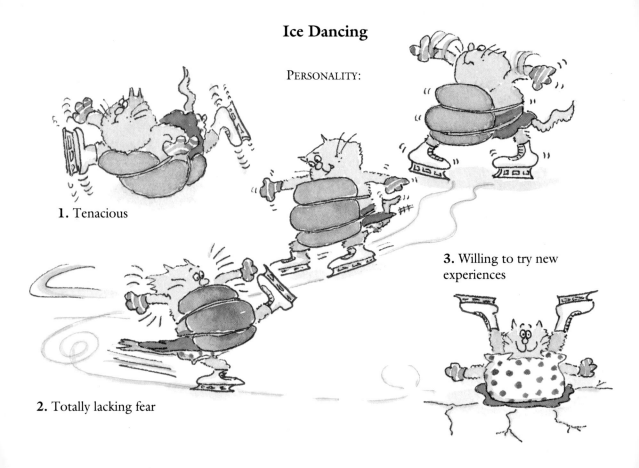

1. Tenacious

2. Totally lacking fear

3. Willing to try new experiences

The Skaters' Waltz

ETIQUETTE ON THE DANCE FLOOR

This is *not* an attractive pose to take up while waiting to be invited to dance.

A friendly, welcoming expression is much more likely to fill your dance card.

It is not sophisticated to sniff someone's rear quarters as a means of introducing yourself.

Grooming your partner's ears is probably best left to the privacy of one's own home.

Etiquette – Fur

Use of White Accessories

If you wear a white shirt, make sure it's a clean one.

White gloves may be old fashioned, but they *always* look smart.

White socks are considered a teeny bit passé by some and are perhaps better reserved for the tennis court and Club Med vacations.

Problem Fur

As a general rule, fur ailments are *not* appealing
on the dance floor. In particular . . .

. . . itching

. . . fleas

. . . severe dandruff

WHERE TO DANCE

Dance can be carried out wherever there is enough space to swing a cat.

It is unusual but not against the rules of propriety to pass (what might otherwise be) a tedious wait at the bus stop by enjoying the rapture of dance. Others in line may even join in, but of course, this must be a matter of personal choice.

WHEN TO DANCE

Dancing is good for the health at any time but is particularly efficacious for the lethargic or melancholy cat.

Scientists have proved that dancing makes you happy.

Circle Dance

Cats come together internationally to create, through their meditative dance, a powerful vision for a better world.

Dancing Around the Maypole

The popularity of this ancient fertility dance has declined
as neutering has become more popular.

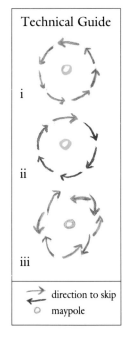

Technical Guide

i

ii

iii

→ direction to skip

○ maypole

MORRIS DANCING

Equipment:
Old cat collars with bells
Sticks
Lots of handkerchiefs (this is
the hayfever season)

Procedure:
Jingle bells
Wave hankies
Knock sticks together

HIGHLAND SWORD DANCE

Equipment:
Any good quality fish knives
will do. If you don't own a kilt,
you can easily make one from
your owner's plaid car rug.

Procedure:

1. Jump up and down. This
helps compensate for heat
lost through draft up kilt.

2. Raise paws above head as if checking foreleg pits for fleas or remnants of breakfast. Continue the jumping.

3. While alternating forepaws between hips and above head, point hind legs in as many directions as possible. Keep jumping.

4. Also spin around on one leg . . . .

Flamenco

Procedure:
Expression is very important in Spanish dances. To find the right look
imagine a strange cat has entered your territory. It is smaller than you.

Remember you've got a tail . . .
don't hesitate to use it.

FRANCE

The Can-Can

Equipment:
Roomy underwear.
Lots of petticoats.
Fishnet knee-highs.

Procedure:
Dance while showing your bloomers as often as possible. Do the split (without your undies splitting, too).

Rip!

Greek Dancing

Ingredients

4 waiters
just off duty

2 tourists
(inebriated)

6 bottles
Retsina

10 bottles
Ouzo
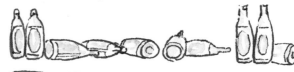

2 dozen
plates

Method

Bake for 4 hours in a beach bar.

GERMANY, AUSTRIA, AND SOME OTHER COUNTRIES

A unique dance is performed in which bare knees and leather shorts play an essential part.

1. Button self in.

2. Slap knees hard.

3. Bite back tears.

5. Slap anyone else stupid enough to do this dance anywhere you like.

4. Slap back legs with front paws vigorously, many times.

6. Take a little time to get a grip on yourself.

Native American Sun Dance

Equipment:
It can be hard to reconstruct ancient ritual dances using modern materials. Do the best you can.

Procedure:
Dance around a pole (representing the sun) for four days. Do not sleep. Do not eat. Do not chase birds. This traditional dance is rarely performed by the modern cat unless it is paid to do so.

Limbo

Use of the tail as a stabilizer during competition limbo is strictly forbidden.

RUSSIA

Cossack Dancing

1. Throw back a glass of iced milk in one swallow.

2. Crouch in excruciatingly painful position and kick back legs in every direction physically possible. Look inscrutable though cool.

3. Leap very high in the air.

4. Land (remain as inscrutable as possible).

INDIA

In the ancient art of Odissi dancing, a story is told through the body's movements. Correct positioning of the front paws is essential . . .

. . . as well as a tranquil and pleasing expression.

Japanese dancers also tell a story . . . through their fans. An open fan may show that the dancer tells of the sun or moon.

A running cat with a closed fan tells us that someone is using a can opener within earshot.

And now . . . a small collection of

VERY MODERN DANCES FOR THE PRE-NEUTERED CAT

This is that stage of cathood
when one is old enough to
be inoculated . . .

. . . but too young
to have kittens.

BREAKDANCING

This is a form of Slamdancing.

Jitterbug, Jive, and Rock 'n' Roll

Paws nonchalantly in pockets, saunter across the room to the
partner of your choice, and growl, "OK, chick, let's hit the floor."

1. Bud simultaneously
combing his pompadour
and jiving with Betty Sue.

2. Bud performing a
technically flawless sneer.

3. Bud carrying out an *incredibly* quizzical glance.

4. Bud handling a tricky moment with faultless aplomb.

HOUSE DANCING OR "RAVE"

Basic Equipment

HOUSE DANCING
Techniques

Hoofers

Is the name given to professional show dancers.

Fred Cat-Hair is possibly the most talented feline ever to shake a whisker.

Accompanied, of course, by the fabulous "Ginger" Rogers.

THE AUTHOR

Viv Quillin, a British citizen, was born in the Pennines, where even the cats need heavy coats and snowboots most of the year round. She is the author of five books, including *The Opposite Sex*, which tramps sensitively through women's sensual experiences. Her cartoons have also appeared in the *Evening Standard*, *Spare Rib*, *Cosmopolitan*, and *New Internationalist*, as well as on postcards, and have been translated into many different languages.

In the hope of acquiring a more cultured sense of humor, she moved to Oxford, England, in 1988.

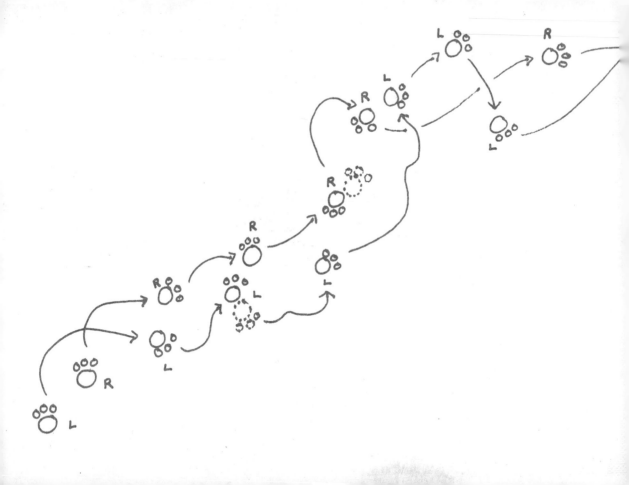